Moses
AND THE BURNING BUSH

Published in Nashville, Tennessee, by Tommy Nelson™,
a division of Thomas Nelson, Inc.
Managing Editor: Laura Minchew
Project Manager: Karen Gallini
Editor: Tama Fortner

Designed by Koechel Peterson & Associates
Digital color enhancement by Carolyn Guske
Cover illustration by Nathan Fowkes

Library of Congress Cataloging-in-Publication Data

Simon, Mary Manz, 1948–
        Moses and the burning bush : a story about faith and obeying God / by Mary
Manz Simon.
        p.   cm. — (The Prince of Egypt values series)
        Summary: When Moses hears the voice of God in a burning bush, he is convinced
to obey God's command to lead the Israelites out of Egypt.
        ISBN 0-8499-5853-9
        1. Moses (Biblical leader)—Juvenile literature. [1. Moses (Biblical leader) 2. Bible
stories—O.T. 3. Obedience.] I. Title. II. Series: Simon, Mary Manz, 1948– Prince of
Egypt values series.
BS580.M6S485   1998
222'.1209505—dc21   98-38569
                                                                                          CIP
                                                                                          AC

Printed in the United States of America

98 99 00 01 02 03 QPH 9 8 7 6 5 4 3 2 1

THE PRINCE OF EGYPT

Moses
AND THE BURNING BUSH
A Story of Faith and Obeying God

by MARY MANZ SIMON

Timeless Values COLLECTION

Tommy NELSON

Thomas Nelson, Inc.
Nashville

oses grew up as a prince of Egypt. But he became a great leader of the Hebrew people and an obedient servant of God. Moses wasn't always a great leader, though. And he didn't even always want to obey God.

Moses lived in the land of Midian with his wife, Tzipporah, and their family. Though he had grown up as prince of Egypt, he had left Egypt many years earlier and was now a shepherd.

One day, Moses led his flock across the desert to the base of a mountain, where the grass was fresh and green. This is what happened on that special day:

"**W**here is that sheep?" Moses grumbled to himself. One of his flock had wandered off. He could hear the tinkling bell on her collar, but he couldn't see her anywhere. Moses followed the sound into a canyon.

"Come back here!" he called after the wandering sheep. "It's too early for this . . ."

$\mathcal{S}$uddenly Moses stopped. He couldn't believe what he was seeing!

Before him, a small bush was in flames, yet it did not seem to be burned by the fire!

Moses stared in amazement. Slowly, he took a step toward the bush, and then another, and then . . .

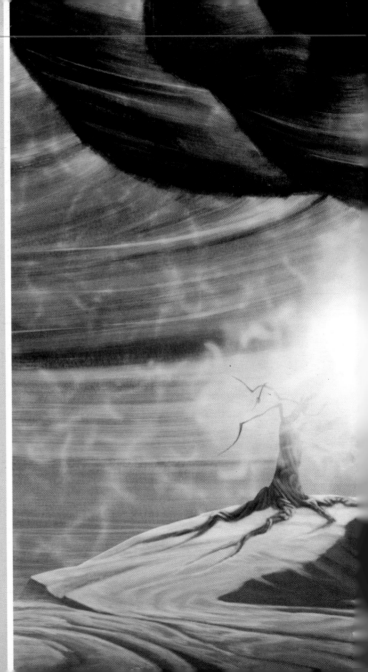

"**M**oses … Moses …" a Voice called out.

The Voice seemed to be all around him. It echoed off the canyon walls. Confused, Moses twisted all around, but he saw no one.

This is a trick, he thought. And he gripped his staff, ready to defend himself.

"Here I am," Moses called back to the Voice.

"Take off your sandals, for the place on which you stand is holy ground," commanded the Voice.

"Who are you?" Moses asked, still looking all around for the source of the Voice.

"I AM THAT I AM."

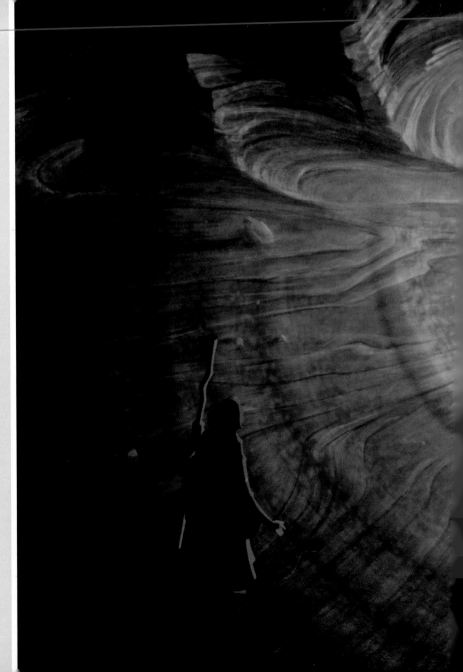

As the Voice spoke, the wind began to blow and the flames of the bush grew brighter. Moses realized that the Voice was coming from the bush.

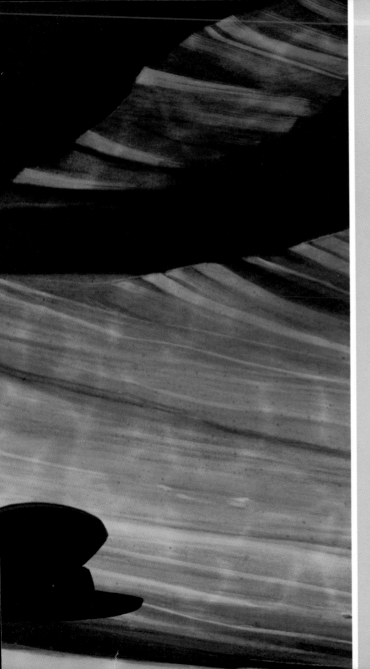

"*I* don't understand!" cried Moses.

"I am the God of your ancestors, Abraham, Isaac, and Jacob."

The Voice was God! Trembling, Moses bent to take off his sandals.

"What do You want with me?" Moses asked.

The wind became quiet, and the
flames flickered and changed shapes
as God spoke.

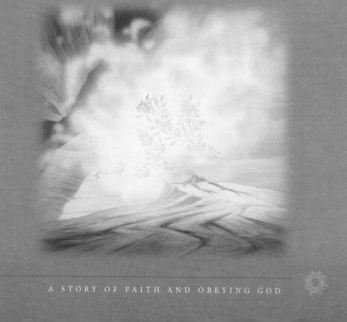

"I have seen the oppression of My people in Egypt and have heard their cry," said God. "So I have come down to deliver them out of slavery and bring them to their Promised Land—a land flowing with milk and honey. And so I am sending you to lead My people out of Pharaoh's country."

Moses backed away from the bush. He did not want to go to Egypt!

"Me? Who am I to lead these people?" cried Moses. "They'll never believe me. They won't even listen!"

"I shall teach you what to say," said God. Then God also showed him two miracles to perform for the Hebrews so that they would believe God had sent Moses to them.

"But I was their enemy," Moses argued. "I was a Prince of Egypt, the son of the man who killed their children! You've chosen the wrong messenger. How can I even speak to these people?"

The flames suddenly flashed and the wind roared with God's anger at Moses and his excuses.

"Who made man's mouth?" God demanded.

"Who made the deaf, the mute, the seeing, or the blind? Did not I? Now go!"

Moses cowered against the canyon wall. He was too afraid to look at the bush. Seeing Moses' fear, God was quiet. He reached out with the wind to embrace and comfort Moses.

"**A**h, Moses," God said gently. "I shall be with you when you go to the King of Egypt. But Pharaoh will not listen. So I will stretch out My hand and smite Egypt with all My wonders. Take the staff in your hand, Moses. . . . With it, you shall do My wonders!"

At last, Moses trusted God and listened with an obedient heart. He dropped to his knees in front of the bush. The wind grew still and the flames of the bush faded away.

$\mathscr{M}$oses stared down at his staff lying next to him. Determined now, he picked up the staff, pulled himself to his feet, and started back.

After a few steps, Moses stopped and turned around to look again at the bush. But now it was just an ordinary plant. This day had begun like any other day in the desert, and now his life—and the lives of the Hebrew people—would be changed forever. Then Moses walked on, ready to obey God.

To Think About

Sometimes it is hard to obey. Moses didn't want to do as God had said and go back to Egypt. He even gave God excuses! Moses had a good life in Midian. He had a wife and a family. Midian was his home now. Besides, it would be much easier to stay in Midian tending sheep, than to go and tell the Pharaoh to free the Hebrew slaves! But if Moses had not obeyed God, the Hebrews might not have been freed from slavery.

Like Moses, sometimes you will be told to do things you don't want to do. For example, you might be told that it's time for bed, even though you want to stay up later. Just as God knew what was best for Moses and the Hebrews, those who care for you know what is best for you. They give you rules to keep you safe, healthy, and happy.

God loved Moses, and God loves you. One way that God shows love is by giving you people to love and care for you. You can show these special people how much you love them and God by trusting them enough to do what they ask of you.

To Talk About

1. Why didn't Moses want to obey God?

2. What are some reasons why you don't want to do what you are told?

3. God promised to help Moses if he went back to Egypt. How does God help you to be obedient?

4. What might have happened if Pharaoh had done as God commanded?

5. When is it hard for you to do as you are told?

6. God appeared to Moses in a burning bush. How do you see God in your mind?

7. God and Moses had a conversation. When do you talk to God?

8. Besides God, whom else should you listen to?